to:

NOW IS the TIME FOR DREAMS.

THE WORLD IS waiting FOR YOU and

the STORIES
you will
TELL.

IT'S Time to GRAB HOLD of the CRAZY, COMPELLING dreams that

WHISPER in YOUR EARS WHEN the lights GO OUT.

It's time To SEIZE the hopes that DRIFT and DAnce in the streets as you Walk by.

HOLD on to the IDEAS THAT elevate your HEART AND electrify YOUR MIND.

PONDER BIG WISHES, CREATIVE PROPOSITIONS, and Adventurous SCHEMES.

It's Time to CONJURE up absurd PLANS, BOLD ACTIONS, and Lofty GOALS.

REVEAL YOUR biggest DREAMS.

UNWRAP them,
AND dusT THEM OFF!

COLLECT ALL the LUMINOUS Thoughts that GLOW INSIDE of YOU.

and SEND them
FLOATING
and SPINNING
into the
WORLD.

ITS time to DROP the SECOND GUESSES,

THE MAYBES, and the not-QUITE-SURES.

LET go of THE HESITATIONS, the procrastinations, AND the WHAT-could-GO-WRONGS.

THROW away your SCRIPTs, YOUR charts, AND YOUR MAPS, with their STRAIGHT LITTLE LINES telling YOU where to GO NEXT.

DITCH the COMPARISONS,

the
BELLWETHERS,
THE Precedents,
AND THE
JONESES.

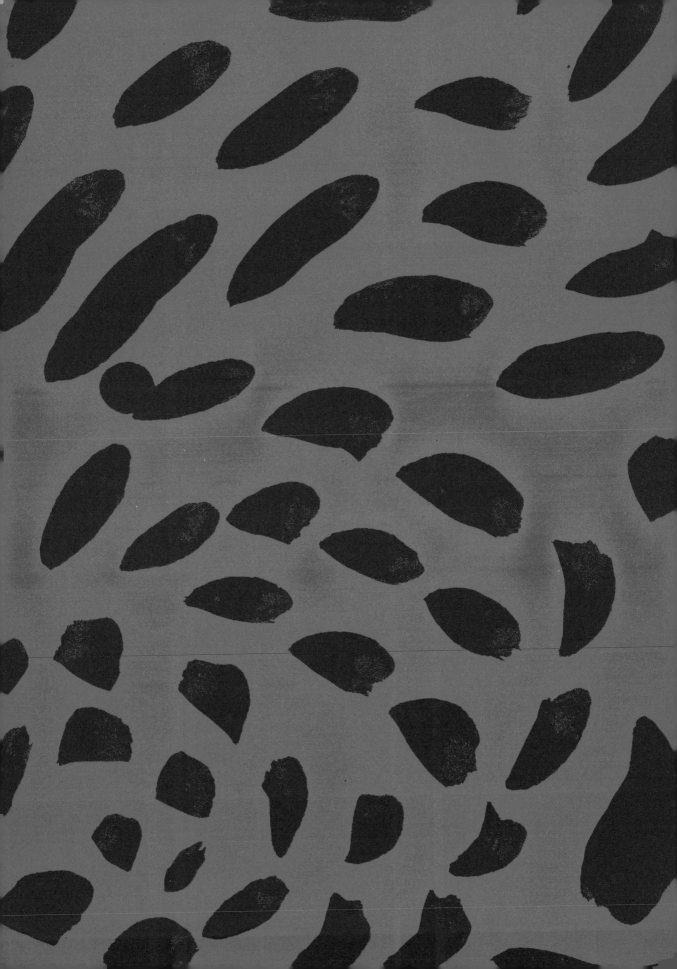

IT'S TIME to VEER OFF COURSE.

GO ON —
SHUT YOUR EYES, AND
FLY BY THE beating
of YOUR EAGER
Heart.

NOW IS the TIME for WILD THINKING and DARING FIRST steps.

This is THE
MOMENT
(the Precise Moment!)
THAT everything
CAN BEGIN.

BUT only if YOU do THE HARD thing.

THE BIGGEST thing...

WHEN YOU LOOK, YOU'LL SEE THAT YOU'RE made UP of a MILLION tiny CURIOSITIES and CONTRIBUTIONS just bursting TO BE REALIZED.

YOU HAVE places LEFT to ExPLORE, projects WAITING To BEGIN,

Successes just AROUND the CORNER, AND _so_ much LOVE to give.

SHOW the MOUNTAINS, Show the SEAS, SHOW THE CRITICS and the Crowds what's BLAZING INSIDE.

YOU ARE your LIFE's ARCHITECT, ENGINEER, and HAMMER

ALL
IN
ONE.

YOU'RE the MASTER of CONTENTMENT, THE CEO of glee, AND

the curator
OF A LIFE
worth LIVING.

You CREATE YOUR OPPORTUNITIES, and you SHAPE the probabilities.

IF YOU WON'T
GIVE YOUR
DREAMS
THE chance
to SOAR into the
WORLD,

WHO will?

REMEMBER, THERE'S NO WHIMSY in the expected, no EXHILARATION in THE easy, and no SPARK OF POSSIBILITY IN What HASN'T YET begun.

THERE'S ONLY time NOW to DO what YOU LOVE.

AND when YOU do what you LOVE. ANYTHING IS POSSIBLE.

BUT FIRST...

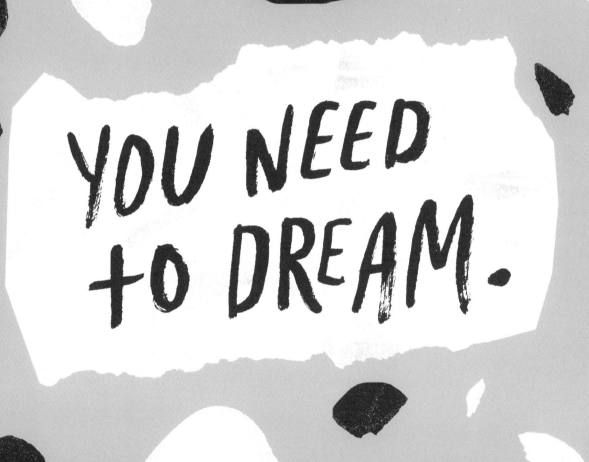

With special thanks to the
entire Compendium family.

Written by: Danielle Leduc McQueen
Designed by: Chris Ballasiotes
Art Direction by: Megan Gandt Guansing
Edited by: Ruth Austin

Library of Congress Control Number: 2017942877

ISBN: 978-1-943200-69-6

1st printing. Printed in China with soy inks.